JOURNEY WEST

I0807526

# Journey West

Jacqueline Martinez

ISBN: 1-55517-426-4

v.3

Published by: Bonneville Books

Distributed by:

925 North Main, Springville, UT 84663 • 801/489-4084

CFI Publishing and Distribution Since 1986

Cedar Fort, Incorporated

CFI Distribution • CFI Books • Council Press • Bonneville Books

*Cover artwork and illustrations by Alex Gonzalez*
*Cover design by Corinne A. Bischoff and Sheila Mortimer*
*Printed in the United States of America*

# Table of Contents


Sundancer . . . . . . . . . . . . . . . . . . . . . . . . . . . . . . .1
A Pinto Pony Named Lightning . . . . . . . . . . . . .3
Sundancer and Buffy . . . . . . . . . . . . . . . . . . . . .5
Buffy Saves Sundancer . . . . . . . . . . . . . . . . . . .7
The Big Decision . . . . . . . . . . . . . . . . . . . . . . . .9
The Journey Begins . . . . . . . . . . . . . . . . . . . . .13
Living off the Land . . . . . . . . . . . . . . . . . . . . .15
Making New Friends . . . . . . . . . . . . . . . . . . . .17
The Farm . . . . . . . . . . . . . . . . . . . . . . . . . . . . .19
The Big Red Barn . . . . . . . . . . . . . . . . . . . . . .21
Grown-ups Visit . . . . . . . . . . . . . . . . . . . . . . .23
Trouble Strikes . . . . . . . . . . . . . . . . . . . . . . . .25
The Wagon Master . . . . . . . . . . . . . . . . . . . . .27
Bear Grows Up . . . . . . . . . . . . . . . . . . . . . . . .29
The Missed Connection . . . . . . . . . . . . . . . . . .31
Jeb Finds a Baby Bear . . . . . . . . . . . . . . . . . .33
A Bear Named Orph . . . . . . . . . . . . . . . . . . . .35
Sundancer Visits a Fort . . . . . . . . . . . . . . . . .37
Moses and Mattie, Runaway Slaves . . . . . . . . . .39
Josh and the Mountain Lion . . . . . . . . . . . . . . .43
Grey Wolf Becomes Mattie's Patient . . . . . . . . . .47
Sundancer and Grandfather Become Guides . . .51
A Log Home in Willamette Valley . . . . . . . . . . .55
Moving into the New House . . . . . . . . . . . . . . .59
Bandit the Raccoon . . . . . . . . . . . . . . . . . . . . .63
The Best Christmas Ever . . . . . . . . . . . . . . . . .65

# SUNDANCER

A beautiful baby boy was born in a Cheyenne Village during a freezing blizzard. His mother, Running Deer, and his grandmother, Walking Woman, did everything they could to keep the tepee warm, but the icy winds seemed to blow right through the thick buffalo hides that the tepee was made of. Because of the storm, only one smoke flap on the top of the tepee was open. The room was filled with thick smoke that made the baby's eyes sting and burn. He did not like the cold or the smoke and he doubled up his tiny fists and screamed out his anger. His grandmother would sing softly to him, trying to comfort her grandson. The baby grew stronger every day and was able to scream even louder. His mother called him Raging Bull.

One sunny afternoon in May, his mother put him outside on a soft buffalo robe. As the sun warmed his naked little body, the baby began to gurgle and coo with happiness. His mother and grandmother put their work aside and went to check on the baby. They were surprised to see him trying to catch the sunbeams with his tiny feet and hands. He was so happy that he even laughed out loud. Grandmother said, "He looks like he is dancing."

Running Deer said, "From this day on, I shall call him Sundancer."

The next time the leaders of the tribe gathered to smoke and to settle tribal affairs, the chief, Sundancer's grandfather, went to his tepee and returned with his grandson. He held the baby high over his head and said, "This is Sundancer. Help me to train him well, because if he becomes wise enough and a good warrior, he will become your future chief."

## A PINTO PONY NAMED LIGHTNING

At that time, Indian children didn't attend school to learn; they were taught by their parents and members of the tribe all the skills required to survive. At first, Sundancer was taught simple things like fishing, swimming, and to safely explore the woods nearby. As he grew older, he learned to build a fire with the flint stone that his mother had given him, to make and use a bow and arrow skillfully and to hunt small game for his mother's cooking pot.

On his fourth birthday, Sundancer was given a strong pinto pony. It was his most prized possession. One day while racing with the other boys in the village, Sundancer's pony finished far ahead of the others. One of Sundancer's friends said, "Your pony is swift like a bolt of lightning." This was to become the pony's name.

Sundancer and Lightning spend many happy hours exploring the woods. They became fast friends and depended on each other. Lightning trusted Sundancer to guide him safely over the little-used trails, and Sundancer depended on Lightning to be fast and sure-footed. They were constant companions, and a deep love and trust developed between the two.

# SUNDANCER AND BUFFY

One cold October evening while out riding, Sundancer heard a pack of wolves closing in for a kill. Being overly curious and never afraid, he raced toward the sound. What he saw made him very angry and not as careful as he should have been. There by the body of its dead mother was a tiny buffalo calf. Sundancer jumped off Lightning and hurled heavy stones at the wolves until he made them run away. He knew that they would be back as soon as it was dark. He got busy collecting wood to build a fire, and to make torches to fight the wolves away from the baby buffalo. The noise and smell of the dead mother buffalo frightened Lightning, and he ran away.

When Lightning ran into camp, Sundancer's grandfather and father grabbed their lances, bows and arrows and left at once to search for Sundancer. They could hear the wolves and Sundancer's angry yelling long before they reached him. They were very proud of their brave offspring as he fought off the hungry wolves to protect the helpless little buffalo.

On the ride back to the village, Sundancer rode behind his father, and Grandfather held the ill buffalo in front of him. When they reached their warm tepee, Sundancer refused to enter unless the baby buffalo was allowed to come inside with him. Running Deer wasn't happy about this at all, but one look at her son's sad face convinced her to say it would be alright.

Grandmother made a thin broth of deer meat and corn meal and using a piece of soft intestine, she fashioned a sort of nipple for the little buffalo to nurse. He was too weak to suckle, so Grandmother squeezed the nipple for him and forced the broth down his throat. Everyone expected the baby buffalo to die during the night. After three days of being fed the nourishing broth, the little buffalo was able to tag along after Sundancer.

Some of the older boys, being jealous of Sundancer's pet, would tease him by chanting, "What a strange thing! A buffalo, only not big enough to be one!"

Sundancer's uncle shouted, "Sundancer, since your unkind friends think you have half a pet, why not give him half a name?"

After thinking about this for a few minutes, Sundancer said, "Thank you, Brother of My Father, for your suggestion. I will call him Buffy."

Buffy spent two winters and a summer with his adopted Indian family. But, as he grew bigger and bigger, he would tear down lodges, eat the garden, and get into all kinds of trouble. Buffy needed to be with his own kind. The second spring of his life, Father and Grandfather led Buffy far away from the village near a large herd of buffalo and set him free. Sundancer was heart-broken, but he knew that it was best for his friend.

## BUFFY SAVES SUNDANCER

While hunting with friends one day, Sundancer raced ahead to chase down a deer. His horse was frightened when a rattlesnake struck out. The horse reared and threw Sundancer to the ground. His friends, not knowing that Sundancer was in trouble, went back to the village without him. It was late fall and starting to be very cold, but Sundancer was not afraid. He gathered enough wood to keep himself warm, and then started to build a fire. His flint stone was not in his pouch. It must have fallen out when he was thrown off his horse. Now, for the first time, he was afraid. Soon Sundancer was so cold that his hands and feet were starting to get numb.

He ran up and down to try to keep warm. Suddenly he heard a thrashing in the trees and prepared his bow and arrow, planning to do battle with whatever was running toward him. He was very happy to see Buffy come thundering out of the forest. The two friends were pleased to see each other. After being petted and having his ears scratched, Buffy stretched out on the ground and snuggled close to Sundancer like he used to do when he was a baby. The two soon fell fast asleep.

When the hunters found Sundancer, he was still alive due to the tremendous heat generated by Buffy's huge body. Buffy came close to Sundancer begging for his ears to be scratched then bolted into the forest. It seemed as if he knew that he had repaid his friend for saving his life so many years ago.

It was the last time the two friends would see each other, but they would always remember the love and fun they shared growing up together—a very brave Indian boy named Sundancer and a gentle buffalo called Buffy.

# THE BIG DECISION

While Sundancer was growing and learning to become a great warrior, two families were making plans to move West. On a cold winter evening in Chicago, Ashley and her cousins Ryan and Travis were huddled around the kitchen table with their parents discussing Uncle Dan's letter from a place called Willamette Valley that was located in the Oregon Territory.

The letter claimed that the land was very rich and free to anyone who would file a homestead and put improvements on it. "The forests," he wrote, "are filled with game, berries, and large trees for building. The lakes, rivers, and ocean are teeming with seafood of all types. The climate is ideal; long, warm summers and short winters with only occasional light snows." Ashley's mom, Michelle, liked this, as she grew up in South Carolina and hated the cold Chicago winters.

The men liked the idea of all the trees needed to build homes, barns, and fences, and that game was plentiful and that the children could go fishing nearby.

Uncle Dan also wrote that the trip in a covered wagon was long and hard. They would need to plan on it taking at least ten to twelve months, but he knew that they would all be happy about being able to own a farm where they could make a good living in an area that someday promised to become a great state.

After much consideration, the decision was made to move. It was a busy spring, preparing for the trip. The houses and furniture had to be sold. Sturdy clothes and supplies were purchased. The funds from the sale of the property were used to buy two large covered wagons and eight strong horses. After buying what was needed for the journey, there was very little money left, so it was decided to live off the land as much as possible. The men would hunt, and the children were to gather any wild fruits, berries, and vegetables available and to fish where there was water.

While the adults prepared for the adventure, the children played games that involved the Indians and different animals that Uncle Dan had written about. He had also suggested that they purchase a dog so that they would be warned if a strange animal or Indian got close to their wagons. He said that a bear would run away from a dog, and that they would be seeing a lot of bears where they were going. They all loved the new puppy Dad bought, and named him Bear because he was large and black.

At last the day to leave Chicago arrived. The wagons were loaded with supplies and the water barrels were fastened to the sides. How excited they all were to be heading West!

As the big wagons went through town the children sat proudly on the high seats beside their parents, smiling and waving to everyone they passed. Sometimes they would yell out that they were headed for the Oregon Territory. Friends and acquaintances would wave and wish them luck on the trip. It was a wonderful morning. It took several hours to reach the outskirts of Chicago, and then, at last, the trip began.

# THE JOURNEY BEGINS

The first night of the trip was like a picnic. The mothers had made fried chicken, beans, salad and cookies the early morning of the departure. That night, after dinner, everyone gathered around the fire to sing songs and tell stories before bedtime.

In the morning, after a very early breakfast, the men hitched up the horses and wagons, and they were on the road before sun-up. The children walked between the two wagons playing games, picking wild flowers and gathering any fruit, berries or vegetables that their moms could use for the evening meal. Bear was forever chasing after them or darting off to the side to run after anything that moved. When they got tired, they would climb into the wagons to rest. It was a wonderful way to live—no school, no work, just the beautiful countryside.

When the wagons stopped for the day, the horses were rubbed down and given a small amount of grain before being turned out to pasture. After that, if the families needed meat, the men would go hunting. If there was water at the campsite, the children would go upstream to fish while their mothers did the laundry downstream.

After dinner everyone went swimming, then gathered around the campfire to dry off. As usual, there was a lot of happy talk about the area Uncle Dan now lived in. It was agreed that they could hardly wait to be there with him.

The children wanted to see some Indians, and Travis kept asking when they would be in the area where bears lived. It had been a long but happy day, and now the soft, comfortable beds beckoned them to retire early. The new day would be filled with many new adventures and would arrive much too soon.

# LIVING OFF THE LAND

The trip was going very well. Everyone was happy and healthy. The decision to move West appeared to be a wise one. Even Baby Taylor, who had been ill when the journey began, had now stopped coughing and was eating like a little piggy. Perhaps it was the warmer weather, the exercise, or her love for Bear the puppy, who was always by her side. Taylor also began to feel very important with the small tasks given to her. She was better than all the other children at finding mushrooms and wild vegetables.

The decision to live off the land proved to be very successful. Before starting the trip, the women purchased a book that explained how and where to find wild foods for people to eat. There were also pictures so that it was easy to identify the plants. The diet was both tasty and healthful. There were spinach, mustard, and dandelion greens, and wild onions to flavor their stews; watercress, which made a wonderful salad, was found on the edge of the clear streams. The prairies offered grains and a vegetable called bread root which tasted almost like a turnip when cooked. There were several different kinds of mushrooms to use in salads and to season with. There were different kinds of berries and grapes and plums to make pies and jams. If a person was alert and followed a wild bee to the hive, he would be rewarded with wonderful honey. The children discovered a grove of black walnut trees. It was great fun gathering the nuts and even more fun thinking of the wonderful cakes, cookies and candy they could be used for. There was also a tree known by the Indians as a Paw Paw tree. The fruit tasted very much like a banana, except that it had lots of seeds. The children loved the fruit and didn't mind the seeds at all. They hadn't had a banana since they left Chicago. In the forests a kind of fern grew that tasted like asparagus when properly prepared.

How very wise it was to live off the land! Space in the wagons could be devoted to sugar, canning supplies, salt, rice, and beans. The wagons were lighter and much easier for the horses to pull this way. Doesn't this sound like fun? Wouldn't you just love to gather your dinner and not have to go to the store?

# MAKING NEW FRIENDS

After traveling for more than a month and not seeing another person, everyone was surprised to have a stranger enter camp one starlit evening. He was a big smiling man with a bright red beard and long hair. Everyone liked him immediately. He accepted an invitation to stay for dinner, but explained that he would have to be on his way soon after the meal. He said his farm was only twelve miles away and that his family expected him home sometime this very night. He said that he had delivered two calves to a nearby Indian village. He said that when he and his wife first settled here, the Indians were quite hostile. One spring after a hard winter, he noticed that several members of the tribe were too thin and seemed to be in poor health. He and his wife gave four beef cattle and some corn and rice to their Indian neighbors. They also taught members of the tribe how to farm certain crops, and each summer delivered two calves so that the chief could build a herd for his tribe. After the gifts, he and his family had been accepted as friends.

The smiling guest had an appetite to match his huge body. He bade the travelers good night and extended an invitation to stay at his farm to rest the animals and to share the produce that he grew on his farm.

# THE FARM

The farm was beautiful. There was a sturdy white house with bright green shutters and a great big red barn. There was an orchard and a garden. The fields were planted in wheat, oats, and corn.

When the wagons entered the lane leading to the house, five boys riding ponies, yelling welcome and throwing their hats into the air, arrived to escort their guests to the house. The boys were very much like their father. They all had happy smiling faces, and some even had bright red hair. Ryan, Travis, and Ashley knew they would have a wonderful time on this visit.

As soon as everyone had been introduced, the boys asked permission to show their young guests the farm. The parents all agreed at once; the children were making so much noise that they couldn't talk.

When the children went out to play, the farmer's wife cautioned them to be certain to remove the pitchfork from the hay before playing on it. She laughed as she told

Michelle and Jamie that she knew the first place her boys would take their guests to play would be the barn. They loved the baby animals, and their favorite pastime was to jump from the loft into the soft, thick stacks of hay below.

# THE BIG RED BARN

The children spent hours jumping from the loft into the hay just as their mother knew they would. At first, Taylor was afraid. The loft was so high up, and the ladder used to climb up seemed to shake when she stretched her small legs to reach the steps. Ashley took her small hand, and letting out a big scream, jumped into the air holding her tight. Down, down, down they sailed through the air. By the time they fell into the soft hay, Taylor was laughing and begging to do it again.

There was a family of soft cuddly kittens that lived in the barn with their mother. They were just six weeks old and walking on legs that were still wobbly at times. They made soft mewing sounds. It was hard to tell if the children loved the kittens the most, or if the kittens loved the children the most. Ashley asked if the kittens had been named yet. When told no, they all decided to help find suitable names for them. One kitten was black with four white paws, so Ryan named it Socks. There was a fluffy white one that Taylor named Snowball. Ashley named a grey-and-white striped one Tiger. Their hosts agreed that they were perfect names. Just then a black one with a white spot on his head came out of the big box they slept in. The farmer's sons insisted that Travis choose a name for this one. After a few seconds of gently stroking the little kitten, Travis decided to call it Ink Spot. They all laughed because the name was cute but didn't really describe the kitten. They all liked the name, and fit or not, it became the kitten's name.

They all loved to ride in the small cart pulled by a white pony called Ribbons. The children didn't go into the house from early morning until time for dinner. There was too much to do, and if they got hungry, they would just climb a tree and pig out on some of the many different kinds of fruit that were ripe. Their wise mothers had made them sandwiches when they left the house to go play earlier in the morning. They managed to always be full and happy.

# GROWN-UPS VISIT

The three women talked, talked, and talked while they baked cakes and pies, made cheese, canned and dried fruit. They also churned butter in a big pottery jar with a dasher. This separated the butter from the cream. It took a lot of time and work, but the children loved to help, especially when they knew how wonderful the butter would taste on biscuits with jam, pancakes and syrup for breakfast, or on a thick slice of homemade bread.

The men inspected the farmer's crops, played cards and learned all they could about farming during the visit. They knew that someday they wanted to own a farm as nice as this one.

It was a delightful visit, but they had to leave. It was

time to start the journey again. There were a lot of hugs, kisses and promises to see each other again whenever possible. There were also some tears as the wagons slowly lumbered down the lane.

When the wagons left the farm, some happy children cuddled two cute kittens, Snowball for Baby Taylor and Tiger held in Ashley's arms.

# TROUBLE STRIKES

The journey had been easy so far, but when the travelers woke up one morning, they found a river too high and swift to cross. The wagons were standing in water and the rain was pouring down. There were frightening claps of loud thunder and brilliant flashes of lightning that promised even more heavy rainfall.

The men decided to move the wagons to higher ground and under a thick grove of trees for protection from the heavy rain. They made a canvas canopy stretched between the tall tree limbs and pulled the wagons underneath it. After building a big fire in between the wagons so things could dry out, they were quite comfortable. They couldn't do anything but wait out the storm. The children taught Bear to play hide and seek. They played games and read while their mothers mended their clothing and their fathers repaired the wagons.

After the evening meal, they would all sing songs, pop corn and make candy. Everyone had fun making taffy. A mixture of sugar, water, corn syrup, vinegar, and vanilla was boiled to a stage where a small amount of candy placed into a cup of cool water would form a hard ball. The candy was put into a dish to cool enough to be pulled without burning their hands. Then the real fun began. Everyone picked a partner, covered their hands with butter, and pulled the candy back and forth between them until it became too hard to pull anymore. The candy was then broken into pieces and placed on a buttered dish. This was the part that Bear liked the best. When the candy was hit with a knife in order to break it into smaller pieces, often some of it would fly through the air. Bear became very good at catching the pieces before they hit the ground. Keeping the children busy and supplying fun things to do as a family helped them to overcome their fear of storms. In Chicago they always felt protected in their well-built houses, but out here in the open, the thunder and lightning were much more threatening.

# THE WAGON MASTER

While they were making taffy one night, a tall stranger rode into camp with a freshly killed deer slung across his horse. He asked if he might share their campfire. He was welcomed and told that he was welcome to dinner if he didn't mind eating what was left over from their meal. He introduced himself as Bill Talbert, a wagon master who was returning home from his last trip. He said that he suffered a bad shoulder due to an Indian arrow and a badly injured back that he hurt when his horse was shot out from under him in an Indian attack. He added that he would miss leading the wagon trains through the wilderness, but he was getting old and missing his soft bed, warm house, and family.

After eating, he asked the men to help him dress the deer he had killed earlier in the day. They cut the meat into chops and roasts to be eaten soon. The rest of the meat was cut into thin strips and placed on a rack near the fire to dry. This would be called "jerky" and would keep for a long time once the process was completed. In order to get the excited children to agree to go to bed, he promised to tell them stories about the wagon train trips to the Oregon Territory.

Bill taught the children and men how to move through the forests without making a sound. He also taught them how to make and use a bow and arrow and how to set traps for small game. He taught them the slight differences in the sounds that the wild birds and animals made and those of Indians imitating those sounds.

Before he left, he called the men aside and instructed them in the best way to fight off an attack on their wagons. He also suggested that once they reached the settlement, the horses be replaced with oxen. True, they would be slower, but were stronger, and Indians preferred horses. He felt that they would all be safer because of the change.

Early the next morning, the trail was dry enough for a horse to make it, but still too muddy for the wagons. The brave adventurous old wagon master bade them all a good trip, thanked them for their kindness, and after warning them to be careful, started on his long trip home.

# BEAR GROWS UP

Bear, no longer a puppy, started to be protective of those he loved. At eight months old, he was very large with huge paws that often caused him to be clumsy.

He loved to go hunting with the men and boys. At this young age, he was very good about flushing game from the bushes and retrieving birds. He liked the water and enjoyed swimming with the children. Once, when they were fishing, the children ran laughing to camp to tell their parents that Bear had caught a salmon. At first they thought that their offspring were trying to play a joke on them; then Bear came into camp dragging a big salmon in his mouth. The fish must have weighed close to ten or twelve pounds, and this was the only way that he could get the catch to his family.

Bear was given much praise and hugs, which made him feel so important that he ran back to the river and caught another salmon that was smaller this time. Bear became a very important part of the families' survival on the journey. He would bark to alert the travelers if anything came close to camp and would chase wild animals away.

One time a porcupine entered the campsite. Bear tried to get it to leave by nipping at the slow-moving animal's hind end and barking. The noise woke the boys from a sound sleep, and they went outside of the wagon to see what was happening. When they saw the kind of animal Bear was after, they tried to make him leave it alone. Bear wouldn't listen. The porcupine was tired of being pestered, so he fought back. Bear ended up with his nose and mouth covered with sharp quills. Poor Bear! He let out yelp after yelp with pain. This woke everyone up. The men removed the painful quills, and the women treated the wounds with whisky to clean and keep infection from setting in. Bear was miserable for days and had a hard time eating. He spent a lot of time in the icy streams and rivers trying to sooth his feverish mouth and nose. Two things he learned from that experience: Never to chase a porcupine, and to always go to his family if he were in trouble.

# THE MISSED CONNECTION

The rain caused a three-week delay. By the time the two wagons reached the settlement where they were to join up with a large wagon train, they were too late. The wagon train had waited for them for almost ten days, but had to move on or they wouldn't be able to cross the mountain passes before the snows were too deep.

Some supplies had gotten soaked and were spoiled, so those had to be replaced before continuing the journey. Then the horses were to be sold and oxen purchased to replace them.

The settlement was dirty and muddy and filled with rough-looking people. The travelers wanted to complete their business as soon as possible and leave.

Funds were practically nonexistent by this time, and the men were very happy with the profit made from the sale of the horses. After the purchase of the oxen, there was enough left over to buy the children some badly needed shoes and a few articles of clothing.

They spent only three days in the settlement before they continued on alone. Everyone had been cautioned not to tell anyone about the trail they intended to take or what their destination was. When returning to the wagons one afternoon, the men found Bear holding a man at bay, refusing to let him leave until someone in the family told him to release the man. He was a shady-looking character, and they were certain that he had intended to rob the wagons. He would have been successful if Bear hadn't surprised him.

The journey to Fort Bridger was exciting. They saw deer, antelope, buffalo, and a lot of elk. Sometimes they saw Indians watching them from a distance. For some reason, they didn't bother the two wagons. Perhaps the old wagon master was right: they weren't interested in taking the slow, awkward oxen or wasting their time to attack wagons that didn't offer enough loot.

The trip went without incident. The days were getting shorter and colder, and everyone was anxious to reach the Fort. It seemed that they had been traveling forever, and they were all tired.

It was a miserable, cold and snowy day when they finally reached the fort. The buildings were very crude, but a most pleasing sight.

They planned to continue on, but the trader at the Fort wisely discouraged this plan. First, the mountain passes would be impossible to travel with the deep snow, and they would surely freeze to death. Second, there was a company of soldiers stationed there for the winter so they should all be safe. There were a few women and children already living at the Fort, and except for the bitter cold, it was a very pleasant winter.

# JEB FINDS A BABY BEAR

A starving baby black bear was rescued by a mountain man named Jeb. Jeb was returning to the mountains after a trip to the Fort to sell the furs he trapped during the winter and to buy some needed supplies. An unexpected spring blizzard caught Jeb miles from his rough cabin. While looking for a place to wait out the storm, he found a small cave.

Once safely inside, he threw down his pack and built a fire with some dry leaves and pieces of wood he had gathered. Jeb was just starting to get warm and could hardly wait to enjoy a cup of the strong coffee he had boiling when he heard a weak whimper. Jeb was surprised. He had thought that the cave was empty.

Now, old Jeb was very tall with huge shoulders and

strong muscular arms and legs. He wore his graying hair and beard long. He dressed in soft buckskin like his Indian friends. He wore comfortable moccasins that allowed him to travel the forest soundlessly. He looked tough, and he was. Still, he was very cautious and grabbed a huge, sharp knife out of his pack before going to investigate the sound. He was very careful when he discovered that the sound came from a baby black bear. Old Jeb was a real fighting man, but he sure didn't want to tangle with an angry mother bear. After searching the cave and not finding a sign of the little bear's mother, Jeb guessed that she must be dead. She apparently had been gone a long, long time. He gently picked the tiny animal up in his arms.

The little bear was cold, so Jeb took him near the fire. He then opened his shirt and put the baby inside next to his own chest to get the little thing warm faster. Still the little bear made weak crying sounds.

Now, old Jeb wasn't completely wild. He liked his strong coffee laced with plenty of canned milk. It just happened that he had a lot of milk in his pack after visiting the Fort. What a lucky thing this was for the baby bear! Jeb, feeling that the small animal was giving cries of hunger, opened one of his precious cans of warmed milk, dipped his finger in it, put it into the little bear's mouth and fed him slowly drop by drop, until he was full and fell asleep nestled against Jeb's warm chest. The little bear adopted Jeb as his parent and followed him everywhere on his wobbly legs. Jeb didn't mind at all, because it wasn't quite so lonely with something cute and lovable to care for.

# A BEAR NAMED ORPH

The Indians started calling Jeb "The Man Who Talks To and Is a Brother To Bears." In a way, this was true. Mountain men for one reason or another chose their kind of life, but it could become very lonely, and Jeb got into the habit of talking to his pet.

Jeb had more or less adopted the bear, and started calling him Orphan. Now, a mountain man doesn't talk very much, so the name soon became shortened to Orph. It seemed to fit perfectly.

The first time Jeb took Orph to Fort Bridger, the people were afraid of the growing bear. The children would cry and hide. The people at the Fort insisted that Orph be chained. Orph didn't like that at all and made sad complaining cries. Jeb couldn't stand to see his friend so unhappy and upset, so he camped outside of the Fort in a tepee with some of his Indian friends who accepted Orph into their home. Orph was never to be chained again.

As time went on, people got used to seeing Jeb and Orph together and realized that Orph was harmless. Finally they would allow Orph into the Fort if Jeb was nearby. The two were visitors to the Fort every spring and fall.

Bears are very smart animals, and Orph soon learned some cute tricks. One was to beg for whatever he wanted. The children soon learned that Orph liked canned peaches. They could get him to sit up and clap his paws if he wanted more. He would also stand up and dance for candy. Whenever Orph was begging, a crowd would gather to watch him perform. The women at Fort Bridger had to hide any canned peaches they had or Orph would end up eating them all! Orph soon became a very unusual bit of entertainment for all who were at the Fort. Word spread far and wide about the gifted bear, and people often came just to see Orph. She was truly missed when she and Jeb returned to their beloved mountains.

When Orph got older, she would disappear for a few days at a time, but would always come back to the cabin and Jeb. The last time Jeb saw Orph, she had two cubs of her own playing in a pile of brightly colored autumn leaves. Orph left her offspring and went to greet Jeb. Jeb petted Orph and went closer to see the cute cubs. The two old friends stood quietly listening to the cold wind that was warning of the coming winter. Orph turned away from her friend and went to her cubs. They ran off into the forest. Jeb knew that this fall, he would be going to the Fort alone. Orph had more important things to do, like caring for her family and finding a safe, suitable cave to spend the winter.

# SUNDANCER VISITS A FORT

Grandfather was taking Sundancer to visit Fort Bridger to learn to trade with the white men. Grandfather also wanted to trade some furs and visit with his friend Jeb, a brave mountain man who had saved his life four winters ago.

On the trip, Grandfather taught Sundancer to say "please" if he wanted something and "thank you" if given anything. To Sundancer, the words were strange-sounding and even more strange to speak.

Sundancer was excited and puzzled by the Fort. The men all had hair on their faces, the wagons had tepees on top of them, and everyone lived in a big corral with strong wooden walls and a big gate that was closed and locked at night.

Inside the Fort, Sundancer saw three children playing a game with a big wooden stick and a ball. The girl had long blonde hair. Sundancer thought he had never seen anything so beautiful, and he wanted to touch it. So he asked, "Please" and stroked the curls gently. The two boy-cousins gave up the game and instantly ran to her side to protect her. At that time Jeb rode up and told the children not to be afraid; that Sundancer hadn't seen hair that color before and only wanted to feel it. Ashley smiled and offered her hand in friendship. Sundancer smilingly said, "Thank you," and handed her a lovely ivory carved necklace made of elk's teeth that he wore around his neck.

The cousins, Ryan and Travis, gave Sundancer a knife that had three blades, a file and a fork. It was to become Sundancer's most prized possession.

Early next morning the women of the Fort were baking bread in the big beehive ovens that were in the front of the trading post. The smell was more than Sundancer could stand, so with his mouth watering, he went to the ovens and when the first crusty loaves were taken out to cool, he asked one of the women "Please," and she gave him a huge slice coated with butter and honey. Sundancer thought it was the best thing he had ever eaten.

The three children became good friends, and Sundancer was very sad when Grandfather said that they must go home soon, as there was much to do to prepare for the long cold winter.

The morning they left, Ashley, Ryan and Travis came to bid their new friend goodbye. They had a gift of two loaves of bread and a jar of peach jam for him. Sundancer was sorry to be leaving, but at the same time excited about all the things he had to tell the boys in the village about what he had seen and learned.

He also knew that come spring, Jeb had arranged with Grandfather to guide his friends and the wagons to Fort Hall, where they would join many wagons with tepees over the top for a trip to the Oregon Territory. It was comforting to know that he would see his friends again soon.

# MOSES AND MATTIE, RUNAWAY SLAVES

Uncle Dan had been to the settlement for supplies. On the way home, he decided to camp out rather than spend the night riding. He liked being in the woods. He had spent a lot of time over the years camping out. The next morning, he had just fixed coffee, fat-back, and pancakes and was ready to eat when he heard his horse whinny. This reminded him that this would be a good time to take the pack mule and his horse to the river for water. He picked up his gun and went to untie the animals.

When he got back to his breakfast, he was surprised to see it was gone! At first he thought it might be a hungry animal. When he discovered a cleverly brushed-out footprint, he knew a human was guilty of taking his food. Not knowing what to expect, he put on his gun belt and also carried his rifle. He traced the prints to a clump of thick bushes. Huddled there was a beautiful black woman with a baby in her arms, two teen-aged boys, and a man. They were clean, but ragged, and looked starved. Uncle Dan knew that they were desperate and could be dangerous. In a kind, gentle voice he asked, "Are you hungry?"

The man's eyes filled with tears as he said, "Yes, sir, we sure are. We haven't eaten in days."

The man's face was a kind one and his voice was gentle. Uncle Dan knew at once that this man was not a criminal. The woman appeared to be very weak, probably from lack of food. Uncle Dan said, "Come, I have more food with me and it looks as if you could all use a good meal." He led them to his campsite and cooked more breakfast. He wondered what they were doing out in the wilderness without a gun, horses, or food. He noticed that their shoes were worn out. They must have walked a long way.

While they were eating, Dan asked, "What can I do to help you?"

They told him a story of horrible mistreatment at the hands of a new owner. Their previous owner had died, so his widow had sold the plantation and the slaves. She went back to France to be with her family. The new owner was very cruel. He had beaten one of the boys so severely that he had been in a coma for days. When he recovered, they had escaped at the first opportunity. He learned that the baby girl was now almost two months old and was born five months after they ran away.

Uncle Dan said, "I've heard about a couple with two teen-aged boys whom two slavers are searching for. There was no mention of a baby. I've got a farm and could use help. I don't have any money right now, but if you want to come with me, I'll protect you and give you food and shelter." He could tell that the woman was too weak to travel, so he suggested that they camp here for another day before traveling to the farm. He also advised them, "Tell the boys to hide if anyone should stop by the camp. It's a couple with two teen-aged boys that they're searching for, not a couple with a baby."

The very next day, two tough-looking men rode into camp. They asked if Dan had seen a couple of runaways with two boys. Dan said, "No, just my man and his woman and their baby." The boys were at the river fishing and Dan prayed that they would remember to hide. The two men were mean-looking customers. Dan wasn't looking for trouble, but if it couldn't be avoided, he had to admit that he liked a good fight. He wasn't going to be unprepared, so he walked over to his horse and lifted his rifle from his pack. Now, Uncle Dan was as gentle as a kitten, but as dangerous as a mother bear if crossed. The men started to climb down from their mounts, but Dan said, "Sorry, friends, but we are leaving. Don't bother to get down."

One man's hand started to reach for his gun, but thought better of it when he noticed how swiftly Dan had lifted his rifle. The stranger decided that he wasn't going to cross this man. He looked as if he could handle any situation successfully. Dan said, "Indians and trappers around here aren't very friendly. If I were you two, I would head for the settlement they call Portland and wait there. If your slaves are still alive, I am certain that they will head for the settlement."

The strangers answered, "Guess you are right, Mister," and they rode off.

Not much later, the boys came out of hiding holding a nice string of fish. Dan chuckled and said, "Sure glad you boys hid. We could have been in a lot of trouble. It is too nice a day to have to waste bullets on an ornery pair like those." He put his arms around the two young men and said, "You are both darn nice kids. I think that we will just have to keep you." This compliment and kindness were just what the boys were hungry for, and they became Uncle Dan's devoted shadows. They followed him everywhere. They tried to talk and walk like him. Dan enjoyed being with them. He came from a large family and now realized how much he had missed the companionship of his younger brothers and sisters.

# JOSH AND THE MOUNTAIN LION

Uncle Dan knew that the woman, whose name was Mattie, was too weak to walk to the farm, so he insisted that she and the baby use the horse. Mattie had never ridden before, so Dan took the reins and walked in front leading the horse.

While walking side by side on the way to the farm, Uncle Dan and the man, Moses, became well acquainted and friends. Moses learned that Dan owned a hundred and sixty-four acres of the most fertile land in Willamette Valley and didn't know very much about farming. On the other hand, Moses had been responsible for overseeing all phases of producing successful crops on a large plantation.

Mattie was very knowledgeable in the use of herbs and healing and nursing. She also knew how to make soap and candles and was a great cook. She could spin and dye cloth and knit stockings and sweaters.

Dan was assured that the boys were excellent workers. Dan chuckled. At this point, this was a little hard to believe. They were constantly wrestling and chasing each other as they tagged along behind.

Baby Rose, whom they lovingly called Rose Bud, was sleeping peacefully now that she was warm and well fed. A few good meals and Mother produced enough milk to fill her little tummy. That plus the gentle motion of the horse had rocked her to sleep for hours. It was well past lunch time when they stopped long enough to cook the fish the boys had caught earlier that morning.

While the boys continued their horseplay, the adults rested for a short time. When the boys came close to a fallen log partly hidden with dead branches and dried leaves, one of the boys, named Josh, heard a sound that reminded him of the kittens he had loved and played with on the plantation. He went to investigate. Thinking he had found a kitten, he stretched out his hand and in a soft voice he called, "Kitty, kitty, here, kitty." What a frightening surprise! Something growled and snapped at his hand. Josh couldn't believe what he saw next. He jumped back and screamed. In front of him was the biggest cat he had ever seen, snarling and baring big yellow teeth. When Josh screamed, Uncle Dan grabbed his gun and ran to the rescue. But the mountain lion was too close for him to use the gun safely. Dan yelled for the boys to face the lion, walk backwards slowly and stare into the cat's eyes until he could safely use the gun. Just as Dan was convinced that the mountain lion was going to spring, she heard one of her babies mew. She bolted off to protect her offspring.

It had been some very tense minutes that could have become life-threatening. Now they all started laughing when the younger brother, Willie, extended his hand and mimicking Josh's voice called, "Kitty, kitty, here, kitty." This made Josh furious and he chased his brother with the biggest stick he could find. He threatened to beat him within an inch of his life if he ever caught him.

As they reached the long driveway to the farm, Moses was surprised to see a building that resembled a small fort. Dan explained that at times he had trouble with Indians and thieves. He also said that as soon as they were settled in and rested, it was necessary for the three males to have guns and know how to use them. In this new country, a person had to know how to protect himself, and a gun was also needed to hunt game. He promised Moses that he would supply the guns and teach them how to use them.

Moses said, "We were never allowed guns."

Dan replied, "Moses, you are starting a new life here with me. You are to be your own man now."

Moses answered, "God bless you. I will never be able to repay you for the kindness that you have shown my family." There were tears in his eyes as he shook Dan's hand.

# GREY WOLF BECOMES MATTIE'S PATIENT

Dan was returning from a successful morning hunting when he heard shots and war whoops. He rode to the top of a ridge to get a better view of the valley below. What he saw made him furious. There were six or seven painted warriors ganged up on a single youth. Dan did not like those odds one bit. He threw his game onto the ground and loaded both of his pistols and his rifle. He raced toward the war party making enough noise for a whole army. When the Indians heard all the gunfire, they galloped away. When Dan reached the young victim, he found him lying face down on the ground in a pool of blood. Dan stopped the flow of blood as best he could, then caught the pony standing beside its Indian owner. Dan tied the youth across the pony's back and headed for the farm.

Moses and Mattie saw Dan coming with the injured Indian and ran out to meet them. They carefully moved the youth inside to their living quarters. Mattie removed a bullet, then cleaned and stitched the wound. She then made a poultice of healing herbs to bind the cuts and gashes. She stayed up all night nursing her patient. For three days he ran a high fever and Mattie was starting to worry. On the fourth day he opened his eyes and tried to get out of bed. He was much too weak to stand and fell to the floor. By late afternoon, he was able to drink a strong meat broth and try to talk.

Dan had turned the Indian pony out to pasture with his stock. Grey Wolf's father spotted the pony while he was out searching for his son. Thinking that Grey Wolf was possibly a prisoner of the big white man, he commandeered a large group of warriors from his tribe to follow him to the farm. When the large band of Indians rode up to Dan's stockade, he warily approached them. Using sign language, the old warrior made Dan understand that the pony in the pasture belonged to his son. Using the same sign language, Dan was able to make the old Indian understand that his son had been wounded and was inside the building. He invited the old man inside, but motioned that the others were to remain outside. When the old warrior saw that his son was alive and being cared for, he made a sign of friendship, went outside, and rode away.

Grey Wolf recovered very fast. He was young with a strong, healthy body. He understood that he owed his life to Dan and Mattie. The three youths each learned a little of each other's language and became fast friends.

Ten days after Grey Wolf arrived at the farm, Josh and Willie caught the pony for their new friend so that he could go home to his tribe.

Sometime later the farm was under attack. It didn't last long because Grey Wolf and members of his tribe drove the warring Indians away. After that, war parties never bothered Uncle Dan's farm again.

Grey Wolf often appeared for a visit. He also had developed a real liking for Mattie's cakes, pies and cookies. He always brought a gift on these visits. One time he came with a cute wolf cub for the boys. She was a soft cuddly little ball of fur that they named Lady. She stole the hearts of everyone at the farm. Grey Wolf explained that her mother had been raised in the Indian village since she was born. Because of this, the young cub should never become wild.

After the evening meal was over, Mattie gave Grey Wolf a chocolate cake to take home. He thought this was a great gift and planned to come for another visit soon.

# SUNDANCER AND GRANDFATHER BECOME GUIDES

On a spring afternoon, Sundancer and Grandfather arrived at the Fort herding three ponies. Ashley, Ryan, and Travis knew that Jeb and their fathers had made arrangements for their young Indian friend and his grandfather to act as guides to lead them safely to Fort Hall in Idaho. The ponies were a complete surprise. Since there were three mounts, they correctly assumed that they were for them.

Ashley chose a small white mare and named her Silver. A bright sorrel that had a white streak in the middle of his forehead was Ryan's choice and was named Blaze. Travis liked the brown horse with a black mane and tail and called it Brown Jug.

The wagons had been packed for days, but there was still much to be done in order to leave the Fort the following morning.

Grandfather rode ahead of the wagons in search of the best trails, to scout for possible trouble and to find the best location to set up camp for the night. The campsite had to have food and water for the stock and a level area for the wagons and the evening cooking fire.

The children had been instructed to gather enough wood for the fire when they first reached the camping area. When this chore was taken care of, they were to care for their mounts. Then they set traps to catch the meat for the next day. If it wasn't too dark, they were to take Bear and hunt for ruffed grouse and other game birds.

They were constantly amazed at the abundance of food this rich country provided. The young rabbits and birds were fried to a crispy brown and served with hot biscuits and honey or jam. The tougher game was used to make tasty stews. The meat was boiled with rice, dried mushrooms and any other vegetable that was available. Grandfather added herbs that he found that day. Those stews would be fit for any king! These meals were prepared in large cast iron pots over the campfire.

They would be on the trail by sun-up each morning. They made good time this way even with the clumsy oxen. Grandfather wanted to cross the rivers before the warm weather melted so much snow that the water would be too swift and deep for a safe crossing.

Sundancer was learning more English and the children more Cheyenne words. Communication with each other became easier each day.

A few days from Fort Hall, they came to a swift river that had to be crossed. The wagons were safely on the other side when the children started to join them. Ashley's mount stumbled and she fell off. Sundancer saw that she wasn't a strong swimmer, so he came to her rescue. Once safe, he tried to tell her the name of the river. He spoke one word: "Snake." Ashley started screaming and climbed up on a big rock. She was still screaming when her father reached her side. Grandfather asked a puzzled Sundancer what had happened. He explained that he had tried to tell Ashley the name of the river. Grandfather instantly understood what had happened. Several times on the trip Ashley had expressed her fear of snakes. He started laughing so hard that tears streamed down his wrinkled old cheeks and it was a few seconds before he could tell others what was causing Ashley to scream.

A very embarrassed Ashley appreciated the humor of the situation. Laughing, she jumped off the rock, pointed to the river and said, "Snake." She then went to the dripping wet Sundancer, offered her hand, and said, "Thank you."

For days the cousins and Sundancer would tease Ashley by pointing to the ground and yelling, "Snake, snake!"

"That's okay," Ashley replied. "I'll get even with you before this trip is over." And you can bet she did!

Two days before reaching the fort, Sundancer and Grandfather bade their friends goodbye. They had now entered Blackfoot territory, and Grandfather had an old enemy in the tribe that he would just as soon not have to deal with at this time. Before they departed, Sundancer and his Grandfather were given a rifle in payment for the ponies and appreciation for their help. This made Sundancer feel very grown up. He would be the envy of all the other boys in the tribe.

When the two wagons reached the Fort, they saw close to sixty wagons gathered there.

That night there was a barbecue. The men had dug a trench in the ground in the middle of the wagon circle. A big fire was built in the trench that morning. When there were only coals left, large rocks were placed in the pit. Then the meat, seasoned and wrapped in sheets of damp canvas, was placed on the rocks. Green limbs were placed over the meat, then another sheet of heavy canvas which was then covered with six to eight inches of dirt. That evening when the meat was removed, it would melt in your mouth with tenderness. The tables were formed into two long rows so everyone was seated in a fashion as to become easily acquainted. There was barbecued pork (which they later learned was actually bear meat), turkeys, and elk. The ladies had prepared beans, rice, and vegetables. The meal was finished with cakes and pies. Afterwards there was music, singing and dancing. For the first time the families realized how much fun it was going to be traveling in a large group.

The next morning, the wagon master and his guides went from wagon to wagon to introduce themselves. The wagon master was a wiry man with a strong face, his skin weathered from constant exposure to the sun and wind. He possessed an air of confidence that was reassuring to all those on the wagon train. One guide was a Blackfoot Indian, the other was part Indian and part black. Both men were rugged in appearance with kind faces. The wagon master let everyone know what rules he would insist be followed on any train in his command. He also appointed certain duties to the men. He was well liked by all.

In just two days, everything was ready, and the wagon train started the journey to the Oregon Territory.

# A LOG HOME IN WILLAMETTE VALLEY

The journey had been a good one with few problems. It had been filled with excitement, fun, wonderful friends and seldom any real danger. At this point everyone was tired and anxious to be in their new homes.

As they started down the long drive they saw Uncle Dan riding fast to greet them shouting, "Welcome! Welcome home!"

The farm reminded the weary travelers of a beautiful park. On the right side of the drive stood three two-storied log houses with huge rock chimneys. They were identical except for the color of the doors. One was red, one was yellow, and the other was dark green. There was a rock planter under the windows where flowers were blooming.

On the left side of the drive, there was a large area planted in grass. This expanse of grass had swings and a teeter-totter for the children. Around this play area was planted a lovely orchard and also grapes and berries.

At the end of the drive was a cul-de-sac with a huge

two-storied barn that boasted a third story that was smaller and reminded them of the look-out at the fort. That was exactly what its purpose was. When Uncle Dan first came here, some of the Indians were quite hostile, so Dan had also built a tall solid log fence around the barn, to protect the stock and himself. He explained that this was the first building to be constructed. It was now home to Mattie and Moses and their brood.

When they had examined the cozy houses that they would occupy, it was hard to realize that Dan had accomplished all this in only five years. The houses boasted three rooms each, a large room for cooking, eating and living, with an upstairs loft with a window at each end, that could be partitioned off to make two sleeping rooms.

When asked how he had accomplished all this, Dan explained, "My good friends Moses and Mattie did most of the work and taught me how to farm as well. Few houses here have windows, but Moses gathered sand and fired it to make glass." He explained that while it was still hot, Moses shaped it into squares, which he later put together with lead to form the windows. "I worked hard, but I had to be taught a lot of things." He gave Moses credit for teaching him the things needed to run a farm successfully. He said, "There's a great story to tell regarding the way Moses, Mattie and I became friends. But that will have to wait until another time. Dinner's ready at my house. It's the one with the green door."

The meal was delicious: barbecued meat, smoked salmon, green beans, corn, hot rolls, cucumbers, tomatoes, iced tea and blackberry cobbler. Never had food tasted so good. They had been seated at a table built by Moses, covered with a cloth made by Mattie. All these nice touches were the last thing the two families had expected to find in their new home in the wilderness.

Uncle Dan thanked Mattie for the wonderful meal and said, "Go home to your family. We can manage the cleaning up." He gave the sleepy children kisses and told their parents to use his house for the night. He said that he would take care of the stock and he turned to go outside. Just before he closed the door, he said, "I am so happy that all of you are here." He closed the door softly and, whistling a merry tune, went out to tend to the stock.

# MOVING INTO THE NEW HOUSE

Getting settled in their homes only took a couple of days. Uncle Dan, Moses, and Mattie had worked very hard to have things as perfect as possible for the new residents.

One end of the large room on the first floor was to be used as a kitchen area. There was even a cupboard with a door! The open shelves below were covered with bright gingham curtains. There was a long table with benches on either side and two chairs for the ends. In the living area of the room there was a long bench that had a high back and arms. It looked very much like a church pew, only with a wider seat. There was also a rocking chair that made the journey with them from Chicago.

The ladies made cushions in a bright print material to match the color of their front doors. They made muslin curtains for the single big window, with tie-backs made of the same material used for the cushions. The rustic log walls, the river-rock fireplace, the bright cushions, a large braided rug and fresh flowers on the table made a lovely, cozy room.

There was a ladder used to reach the sleeping loft. A curtain in the middle of the room created two sleeping areas, one for the children and one for their parents. The children's quarters had a bunk bed and their parents' had a wide bed. The beds were made with a strong wood frame that had small holes spaced approximately two inches apart. Rope was woven across and lengthwise of the frame. Then a soft feather mattress was put on top of the rope. This made a very comfortable bed. Clothes were to be stored in trunks and hung on pegs until there would be time to build closets.

This was a very busy time. Even with the extra helping hands, the day began before sunrise and ended long after sundown. The corn had to be gathered, the wheat and oats and rice winnowed to separate the chaff from the grain. Vegetables had to be canned, dried and some put into the cellar. Those put in the cellar had to be cleaned and placed on a bed of dry straw. Fruits and berries were made into jams and jellies.

No one minded the hard work, because it meant that there would be an abundant supply of food to last until the next crops were ready to harvest. Hay also had to be cut and stacked for the stock.

When all this had been accomplished, it was decided to celebrate by having a picnic beside the Willamette River. They were aware that the weather was becoming too cold for any more outings like this. The days were getting shorter and mornings usually started out with a light drizzle.

It was a wonderful day, with games, good food, and lots of just getting to know each other better.

Before packing up to go to their homes, Uncle Dan asked everyone to gather around the fire. He said that he felt that it was very important that they all know the story of Moses, Mattie, and their children. He said he wanted them to make a promise to do certain things for his friends should anything happen to him.

# BANDIT THE RACCOON

While the children were out helping their fathers survey the land they were going to claim, they found an abandoned nest with two baby raccoons in it. Only one was still alive. Something must have killed their mother. The baby's pitiful cries were weak. Ashley couldn't stand to leave the helpless little animal to die. She gathered his shaking little body up in her arms and wrapped her warm sweater around him. When she reached the house, she took the tiny raccoon to Mattie's home and asked her to please use her nursing skills to save his life.

Mattie was so successful that in a short time the little coon was very much alive and filled with mischievous energy. He had thick yellowish gray fur. His long tail had black rings around it. His face had black mask-like markings around the eyes. The children named him "Bandit" because of the mask, and because he constantly stole and hid things. He would hide behind things, then jump out at them and hitch a ride. He drove Bear and Lady wild chasing and biting their tails. He could climb anything. He had little hands that looked almost human, and he washed them as well as his food before he would eat. He liked to climb Uncle Dan's tall frame and steal some of the chewing tobacco he kept in his shirt pocket. When Bandit was angry with his human family, he would clinch his little hands into fists, dance up and down and screech his displeasure. I'm sorry to say this happened quite often. Everyone thought he was so cute that they would roar with laughter and this made Bandit even more angry. After one such display of anger, Ashley gathered Bandit up in her arms and gently petted his neck to soothe him as she said, "Bandit, I love you. How did we ever get by without you to keep us amused?"

# THE BEST CHRISTMAS EVER

A wild wind whistled around the cozy log cabin and rain pounded the roof. The children were all asleep in the loft, as Ryan and Travis had spent the night with their cousins. Their mothers were sitting near the fireplace drinking rose-hip tea and making ornaments of brightly colored material for the Christmas tree. Dan and Ricky were on their way to the settlement to purchase supplies and any gifts that they might find. Moses and Tom were in the barn making sleds to surprise the children with on Christmas. Mattie was in her quarters knitting sweaters and gloves for the children, scarves for the women, and stockings for the men. Rose Bud was fast asleep and the boys were huddled near the fire reading.

Jamie said, "I hope Dan and Ricky reached the settlement before the storm hit."

Michelle answered, "Me, too, but Dan is a capable woodsman. I am certain that he will find some kind of shelter."

As the two women worked, Michelle asked, "Do you realize that it has been almost two years since we received Dan's letter and decided to join him in the Oregon Territory? Are you ever sorry?"

Jamie replied, "No! I never want to live in a big city again. I am certain that we have never been healthier or happier."

Michelle said, "What do you make of the promise to Moses that Dan wants us to fulfill if anything should happen to him?"

Jamie stated that in light of all Moses and Mattie had done for all of them, they certainly deserved to have a good piece of land. Michelle agreed.

Dan and Ricky had reached the settlement a couple of hours after the storm hit. The streets were already knee-deep in mud. The only shelter they were able to find was in a damp tent with rows of hard cots set up side by side with no blankets or pillows. Dan felt that they would have been better off in his beloved woods. The settlement was a madhouse of activity and the air was saturated with foul smells. Dan wanted to conduct their business early and leave for home in the afternoon. Ricky felt the same way.

When the two men arrived home, they were pleased to be greeted with lovely wreaths on the doors, and Christmas trees decorated with strings of white popcorn, red berries, and bright cloth ornaments. Dan said, "You will never know how good it is to be home. We are all so lucky."

The following morning, the men went hunting while the women baked. Christmas was just a day away.

Christmas Day arrived with snow. The excited children, after opening presents, were warmly dressed in their new sweaters and gloves. They were out the door to play with their new red sleds. Lady and Bear had a great time chasing after them.

Two of the long tables were placed end to end and were piled high with delicious foods: game birds with corn bread stuffing, green beans, mashed potatoes, corn, hot rolls, pumpkin and apple pies. The meal was a wonderful way to end a perfect day. Santa brought Taylor and Rose Bud each a cuddly rag doll. Ashley got a lovely gold locket, Ryan a gun of his very own, Travis the guitar he wanted, Josh a pony, and Willie the fishing equipment he had asked for.

Uncle Dan poured the adults a glass of wine, and even the children were given a swallow for this special occasion. He raised his glass and said, "Let us all drink to the very best Christmas ever and to the best possible life here in the West."

-The End-

# About the Author

I was reared on a ranch in Arizona. My mother was a petite Teddy Kosloff ballerina and my dad was a big Scotch Irish farmer. They tell me that as a child, I wanted to become whatever was exciting to me at the moment. If I went to a rodeo, I wanted to become a rodeo performer, an actress, a nun and when I attended a circus, I wanted to be a lion tamer.

When I was 23 years old and a mother of two beautiful little girls, I decided I needed to complete my education, so, I enrolled in Stanford University. My husband had health problems as the result of being in World War II and it was necessary for me to continue working. In answer to my prayers, I was offered a job modeling for the Estelle Compton Agency in San Francisco. I made arrangements with Gus Gustanfon who owned a drive-in located on Bayshore highway to work on Friday and Saturday nights from 6:00 p.m. - 2:00 a.m. and Sundays form 1:00 p.m. - 7:00 p.m. This gave me the week free to go to Stanford and to model. It was difficult, but, I made it until a round of tonsillectomies put an end to my education just three months away from my graduation.

I then went to work in real estate because I had an aunt and three uncles in that profession, in the state of California. I was successful in that business and stayed in it in the state of California for 27 years.

My baby daughter was ill for years with a bad heart and she passed away in 1989. I often had her five children to care for years at a time, but, it was very rewarding. The children have all matured into well-educated, responsible adults. I am very proud of each and everyone of them. In 1992 we retired from San Diego California to Idaho Falls, Idaho. Finally, forty-one years later I had time to use my creative writing course and am able to write. I have just completed a novel and am doing research for another book of children's stories.